GW00597247

Nasty, British & Short

Nasty, British & Short

Ann Alexander

PETERLOO POETS

First published in 2007
by Peterloo Poets
The Old Chapel, Sand Lane, Calstock,
Cornwall PL18 9QX, U.K.

A catalogue record for this book is available
from the British Library

ISBN   978-1-904324-38-6

Printed by 4word Ltd,
Unit15, Baker's Park, Cater Road, Bristol BS13 7TT

ACKNOWLEDGEMENTS

Many of the poems within these pages have appeared in literary magazines, including *Scryfa, The Frogmore Papers, Mslexia, Envoi, The Interpreter's House, Magma, The Literary Review*, and *Reach*. 'The mystery of the place' was part of Radio 4's National Poetry Day celebrations in 2003. Other poems have appeared on websites such as BBC2, *Birmingham Words*, and *The Poetry Library*. 'After all that' was placed third in BBC's Poem for Britain, 2003, and was published in Daisy Goodwin's *Essential Poems for Britain (and the way we live now)*.

For Maurice and Lucy, with love and thanks

" . . . the life of man, solitary, poor, nasty, brutish, and short."
Thomas Hobbes

CONTENTS

After all that

On Parents' Night, in the crumbling hall
of the Empire Street Infant and Junior School,
a discomfort of strangers met to discuss
their children's future.
    No one knew
quite why the awful fuss broke out,
but suddenly *names* were flying about –

twelve Brummies, eleven Cockneys,
ten Taffies, nine Jocks, eight Micks
seven Blacks, six Krauts,
five Scousers, four Frogs, three Pakis,
two Chinks and a Corn

were cussing each other, over their children's heads.
All of a sudden, a parent said:
I'd kill for a decent cup of tea.
    Later,
seventy eight mums and dads went home.

Clean break

After the strife and the cold *stuff you*
I vacuumed him out of my life
with my Dyson DC07, Mk II.

The Dyson's moans drowned out my own
as I watched his motes and beams fly round
the polycarbonate plastic drum.

I sucked the bugger in! I seized
the see-thru serpentine flexible hose,
sought him in every corner and crease.

And all the dirty things he said
were caught by the cyclone-action spin,
and filtered out. I wanted him dead –

Dust to dust. Smooth textured, fine.
I emptied him out on the compost heap,
with the half finished bottle of wine.

In the wet-faced hours of the night

considering love, or the lack of it;
on-the-one-hand-this,
on-the-other-hand-that –

in these steep and solitary hours
come the raw questions.
And sorrow surfaces as tears,
and moonlight finds me, stretched
like some trussed Gulliver, among
the little, scampering, bossy needs of life;
the pinpricks of the new day's coming cares.

And yet.
The day will dawn. A bird will sing.
A hundred different clichés spring to life.
Even in this January,
light, unstoppable, will show
the old camellia, up against the wall,
a shout of lipstick red.

Three men on a bench

Mac's the first to come. Sags, sits,
adjusts his bags, his dog. Half past breakfast.
Already broken a promise, three by-laws, wind
from the north, and he reckons it's Friday.
The tin in his hand, corpse cold -
yet heat rips through him as he gulps
the liquid, jerks to puzzled life.
Two cans and a roll-up down

the path comes Dan, shivering hot.
They grunt acceptance, hunch, eye out
for that mad bastard Diz who's late,
or else them bastard cops; that tosser,
sat here yesterday on this, their bench,
and wouldn't shift - *I pay my tax, do you?*
he said, although they eff him, blind him, kick
this bleedin habit soon -
Diz shuffles up, grunts, stops, sits.
Seven beers and two joints down
with all the world. At two they sleep,
crumpled on the seat; three guys, one dog,
waiting for Bonfire Night.

Nothing left but anger, and this bench.
Don't matter if the brass plate on it says
in memory of Ethel Jones, who loved this view.
They glare through blear at tennis courts,
houses, cafes, all the things they never had
the knack for: wives, jobs, kids, health, home
is this bench now.

Our bench.

Three men wake up, stare down the world.
Our bench.   Not yours nor effin Ethel's nor
some other bastard's.   Ours.   You heard.
Now give us your bastard change

is not an option, any more.
Move on, the copper says.
Move on now lads. Move on.

Bog Lady

I have come out of the peat to this white place,
to show my burnished skin, my tufts of ginger hair –
dreadlocked, beaded, stiff with dirt.

I was a stranger in that other time, lost on the tracks
that snake the wet. I crossed their boundary, and so
they took me, withy-bound, to meet my four slow deaths.

Since then I've slept and slept. I am Persephone,
dragged out of hell, reeking with different rules
which I must now forget. And learn instead

the ways of drying air, hushed tongues, the shrink
from difference, laws of other and strange.
what's left curls in disarray. I am in no man's land.

They found six seeds inside my gut. They speculate.
A wet place waits, bordering our worlds,
where they will float me soon
to meet another kind of death.

War Orgy

It begins politely enough:
      you sure you're ready for this?
      Perhaps we shouldn't, after all?
Long hours of nervy preparation,
buying time. Talk of need and want.
How good you'll feel, afterwards.

Flirtatious skirmishes at the border
take a lifetime. Smothering your fear,
you close in, step by cautious step
as tension mounts. Blood's up.
The darkness falls, and you can't help yourself –
you're in it up to here; eyes burn, skin pricks
and pulses thump – everywhere
confusion, noise; the stink of tangled flesh.

Now you're into the hard stuff.
Handcuffs, chains; gloves off, masks on,
knives, whips, bruises, pumping blood –
no longer know who's who or why;
is that a woman, child? Too late to ask.
You're blind and deaf to all except
your need, your tom-tom heart.
Who knows if that sharp sound's
a yelp of pain, or of surrender?
Don't much care. Staring bodies slide
like Scuds towards the only end:

the shuddering, shivering thrill
of total bloody victory. You crow,
a farmyard cock above a heap of flesh.

      Afterwards,

a long time afterwards,

you're gazing at the ruined landscape, spread
on what once passed for normal.
Mumbling your excuses, your goodbyes,
you whisper *never again*. Clean up the mess.
Patch the wounds. Arrange the shattered house.
Seek those responsible for this or that excess.
Dominator, dominated, both creep home,
to shamefaced days, a kind of reparation.
Count the cost.

Who made this rose?

God, sings my soul. God made this rose.

The rational me shouts:
No! The gardener made the rose
and all the other roses since
the first flat smudge on the arching briar.
The gardener made the rose.

Before the gardener came?
The roses made themselves,
back to the alien micro-life
on the hot primeval rock.
The would-be roses made this rose.

And who, my soul enquires, do you suppose
made that alien micro-life,
on that primeval rock?

Why, God, I say.
I can believe in a God like that.

We have ways

To every dog and every man,
one bite.
The lately-come who moved next door
bit twice. Of course we bit back, right?
Natural justice. Self-defence.
When in Rome, and all that shite.
Still they didn't cotton on.
She mouthed off, and he mouthed off,
threatening this and threatening that –
any wonder war broke out?

This is how us locals fight.
First, the silence. Turn the back.
Show the shoulder.   Moon the arse.
The poison pen. The window smashed.
The kid's eye blacked. The drainway blocked.
The silent phone calls in the night.
The tyres slashed. The garden trashed.
The goldfish squashed. The shed alight.

Still the buggers stuck it out.
They found us locals don't give in:
the dead rat lying on the grass,
the music blaring out till dawn,
the shouted insults as they pass,
graffiti sprayed across the lawn –
sod off back to whence you came.

What d'you think? They called the police.
We had to laugh, they sent some lad.
He asked the questions, we said nowt –
but now they'd made us hopping mad.
This was breaking all the rules.

Well out of order, understand?
You never get the coppers round
in England's green and pleasant land
(unless it's someone fiddling kids
or murder, or your car's been nicked,
something *seriously* bad).

Only got themselves to blame.
See her grin, the silly cow?
We had a meeting, my front room.
We got a gun, don't ask me how.
We showed them how us locals win.
We shot the dog.
They're moving, now.

The sod it years

Here at last, the *sod it* years,
when *bugger it, why not?*
flies to the tongue
as quickly as chocolate cake.

In the years of *if not now, then when?*
you might as well have it,
the dress or the fag or the man
or the bet on the nag.
You might as well grow it,
the spare tyre, the beard,
the hair in the ears.

Oh, the hell with it! years
are such a relief: no more holding back.
Just do it, we say to an audience of one,
as the days turn to dust
and our bodies grow slack.
Who needs to be sober?
Who's looking at us?

The mystery of the place

We can believe the thatched roof
they tell us capped these round huts.

We imagine the rough room
where they claim the pig lived,
waiting his iron time.

We acknowledge the flat stone
where they say the fire burnt,
put our noses to it, sniff the scorch;
stoop through doorways made for smaller bones.

In the midden, they found grains,
shards, skulls, the trace of fish.
And we are told man lived here well enough,
on this hard hill, fine-tuned to danger.

But the fogou. That they can't explain.
Thirty feet of tunnel snakes beneath
the hill's curve, a round room
to end it, like a question mark.

They say: some people think – and offer up
simple explanations. Hiding holes,
storage rooms, some ritual, perhaps.

Two thousand years from now
will someone stand here, staring at
what's left of that stone information hut
set neatly by the stile below,
wondering why?

On land, he is a chapel man

At sea, he wears a red scarf at his throat.
He won't wear green. He touches wood.
Never says thirteen. He will not sail
on Friday. Will not sail
if he should pass a vicar, or a nun.
He cannot sail
if crow or owl lights on his boat.
He never sails
with Finn, or woman. Will not talk
of rabbit, pig, or rat. Carries in his coat
a bone, a ring, a piece of purple glass.
Takes nothing from the sea, but fish.

    Landed, he's a chapel man,
    sings like a burly angel, in the choir.
    Landed, he's a family man,
    digs his garden, mows and trims the grass.
    Landed, he's a social man
    and likes his seven pints.

He never whistles, when he is at sea.
Had a mate once, whistled up a wind;
the sea bucked underneath them like a whale
shaking some irritation from its back,
and tipped him overboard. All the wild night
they searched, crying his name.

Next day rose calm. The skipper put
a candle on a slice of bread,
floated it on the waves, to comfort him.
He thinks of this friend, as he ties
his optimistic knots,
his sheepshank, clove hitch, Turk's head, true love.

On land, he is a chapel man,
and wishes to be buried there, one day.

Man Friday

We catch sight of him as we sail by,
a head down man-speck
foot-printing the shore, then veering off
into the dark interior, searching for his tribe.

He spoke their language once,
but now his Anglo-Saxon-twisted tongue
chokes on their consonants.
He sees their eyes roll skyward,
knows they're dreaming of
the taste of him, and how
his stranger's head will look, shrunk small.
It's time to leave.

Torn between two ways of being,
head in one place, heart elsewhere,
what can he do but pace
the wet, white shore as if it were
a prison yard, grieving for the man
who suddenly appeared, knew
the workings of the sun, and yet
could never learn to catch a single fish,
in all that teeming sea.

Eyes blind to our small boat,
he scans the sea for ships that bring
that other kind of man,
the one who found him, named him, left,
and promised to return.

When you show up three days late and smirking

with another shed-load of daffs
from the florist who must think it's Christmas –
and you mouth the well thumbed words
through the beer-smelling hole in your face,
reach out a practised hand for mine,
and whoops you're over the threshold,
reading your watch and oiling your way
to the bedroom door,
loosening your tie as you go –

and you fall on the bed like a force of nature,
say *come on babe, don't be a drag,*
and toe your shoes off your squid-cold feet
and hold out your arms
as if I were the answer and not the question –

and my insides curdle, my legs stumble,
my lips find your lips, not just to shut off
the sound of your voice –

that's when I know it's love.

So far, Soho

Are you
heterosexual, homosexual, phonesexual, asexual,
metrosexual, transsexual, polysexual, cybersexual?
Onanist, fetishist, abstainer, no brainer,
one of the I-should-be-so-luckies,
or one of the thou-shalt-nots? Are you

promiscuous, fastidious, daring, a dabbler,
professional, pretender, caring, a groper?
Into underwear, the underage, overage, bondage,
your neighbour, your neighbour's wife,
his sorry ass, his hairy ox; your sister or your brother,
or your poor deserted ex? Promise me

no claptrap, comeback, backlash, mishmash,
burnmarks, burnouts, lockouts, whiplash,
set ups, stuff ups, shoot ups, shoot outs . . .

Actually, do you mind if we don't?

The house remembers

At night the house walks about itself.
Windows rattle to windows, turn reflective.
Boards creak to walls, leaning against
their own weight as the house remembers.

Oh yes, the house is discreet enough by day.
Self-effacing, there for our needs,
blending to the background like a butler.
But come the night the house remembers –

Recalls the cliff its granite blocks
were blasted from, the sand that made the glass,
the forest where the doors were born.
The sedimentary slate looks back, longs for
its natal mud. Even the oil that made the paint
acknowledges a salty ancestry.

Scissor, paper, stone – this construct
forced to false, unnatural form,
was torn and blasted, boiled and knocked,
sawn and dredged to life; tacked together
long before my birth. I'm nothing to it,
last in a line of users.   The grit in its eye.

One day the earth will shudder, and the sky will fall;
and as the dying ages come and go
the house will burn and break, return once more
to forest, cliff, and sea, and silver shore.

The house by the crem

What a bargain. We bought it.
Mock Tudor, five beds,
room for the kids and the dog.

We sat on the shaved lawn, smoked grass,
backs to the view.   Ignored
the chimney pointing skywards,
stately limos crawling down the lane,
choked with flowers and things
it's better not to think of.
Don't dwell on it, we said,
Pass the bottle, baby. Fill the glass.

Time walked slow behind our high hedge.
You wouldn't know the other place was there.
But in the night we smelt it.
Smoke seeped in and left its mark
on washing, children's toys.
We kept the windows closed. Drank gin.

When autumn came,
curiosity did for the cat. Soberly,
we ventured through the gates,
crept down the ordered walks,
where signs advised: *no spitting, please*
and *take your litter home.*

No mention of the d-word, here:
just scrawled acknowledgments
of illness bravely borne,
and crow-black figures, grieving.

But oh! The roses!

The explorer explains

So why did you go?

A restless gene
told me this can't be all
and an answer lies
in the untrodden snow,
the Gobi, the outback,
the ocean, the view
beyond the garden wall.

And when you got there,
what did you find?

More of the same.

And when you came home
was there peace of mind?

Only more of the same.

The coming of colour

We've got the colour now, said Mrs Jones
eyeing our black and white.
Dad flushed, flashed her a look.
Mother screwed her mouth up tight.

Nuff said. That Saturday, we trooped
to town and got our own,
not bought outright, but on the knock.
Nineteen inch, fifteen quid down.

It sat in state. We crouched around
like people sit in church. All rapt
attention. Then Dad switched it on.

There comes a time
when winter's monochrome gives way
to riotous spring; when certainty's plain
black and white (cops/robbers, good and bad,
that sort of thing) takes on a million shades
of maybe. This was that moment.
No more wrong and right.
Out went the old, and in came fireworks night.

Change was instant, like the coffee that
you didn't percolate. The fellow reading out
the news in dinner jacket, that posh woman's hat,
those vicar chaps who preached goodnight
seemed silly now, in colour. Shove the lot,
we thought, but didn't like to say
(much too polite).

The clothes love wears

Not the scarlet, black
and slippery kind
you find in the small ads,
sent under plain cover.
Those are the clothes
sex wears.

Not the sharp suit,
shoes reflecting back
your own face.
Not the cantilevered bra
the basque, the dress
concealing and
revealing nothing:
those are the clothes
seduction wears.

And never the old blouse
that might have belonged
to your mother, the worn jeans.
Those are the clothes
marriage wears.

Love is naked as a newborn;
walking blind in a world of eyes.
And after love, it's sackcloth or silk,
nothing in between.

The back end of a pantomime horse

It's a start, said my mum.
Ought the girl? cautioned Gran,
alert to the dangers of running about
with my head on a man's backside.
Trust you to be different, fretted my friend,
who'd like to be Kylie, or Catherine Zeta Jones.

All I could hear was the crowd,
all I could smell was the bum in front.
All I could see was the dirty stage,
his look that said
I am the horse, you are the horse's arse.

It rankled – I grew reckless. Tried a few
impulsive kicks. Crossed my legs
at the ankles. Did a pirouette,
held my tail out, straight as a flag.
The crowd adored it, roared their delight.

Then I thought, why not try for
the real thing? I studied the horse,
waiting for Curtain Up. Gave her a name,
lived on water and grass. My legs
grew fur. I kicked off ersatz hooves,
stripped bare. Dreamed myself out
on the plain, blonde mane streaming,
or dripping like willow, down to the
clear pool. I longed to feel
green in my throat, never a soul
astride my back, never a heel
in my heaving side, never a stick
nor a bit nor the pull of a rein.
The front end put his hoof down. Said

It's the not knowing.
Front legs going one way, back the other.
He played the horse in the old manner,
flower behind one ear, hat on his head.

The rest you can guess. One of us had to go.
At pantomime time, I wander the moor
and think of him, knowing that over the rise
my lost herd roams, lifting their heads as one,
calling me home.

Summering, southwest

Sudden and pungent as smoke,
the travellers roll up, stop travelling.

Slap in front of some world-class view,
they scuttle their vans, sign on,
drift to littered doorways on the street –
parishioners, claiming their pew.

Ringed through noses, lips, cheeks;
dogs on string, packs on backs,
in many-layered motley mess,
they lurch from Threshers to the DSS.

We locals, hosts to the working world
scratching a living in small hotels,
give hard-won coins to keep at bay
their so much worse reality: cold light of day.

We stare. The travellers hardly notice us.
scarce out of childhood, hear them speak
in tongues of cities up the line – Welsh lilt,
the Rizla rasp, Glasgow in a ragged kilt.

They don't look up as coin hits cup,
just nod as we cough up;
their lives unravelling, on hellish holiday.

Fear finds them in the end.
One shivering day, they run to mums
in Morningside, Chalk Farm, Crouch End.

Why deep sea fishermen can't swim

Ashore, they pour down pints
in quantities that beggar all belief,
empty their pockets of the pay-off wad,
crawl home, anaesthetised
against the knowledge of what waits.

On shore, they sing, shout,
love after a fashion. All things fine
have gone the way of childhood, in this town
where rockbox houses cling to cliffs.

On land, they smoke and snort
as much of this or that as they can score,
in sideways-shifty pubs along the quay.
Trying not to think about the way
the black Atlantic flings a boat about,
as they, sober as Witnesses, are taught
the truth that force ten weather teaches men;
sleeping-waking fully dressed on boards,
soaked through and shaking,
all for a weight of fish.

And if the seventh wave should catch them
and they tumble into that far
notch-above-a-bollock-freezing sea,
they know their curse would be
to know the way to swim,
when truly there's no way to swim,
no hope, no guiding star.

Summer with Grandpa Coal

Some holiday. No sandy beach, or sea.
Only the rich, sour reek of coal,
black mountains of it, scree,
tumbling with the scrambling child.

A wooden ladder, tacked
to the stable wall, Up there,
with hay and stacked Victorian tat,
black cobwebs, lay a thousand
scattered bills, *one ton of brights*
or *coke*, or *slack*, hard words
rekindling fires long since grown cold.

Turfed out after breakfast, told
Don't come back till lunch!
We got so greasy black,
and no-one cared. Out back,
behind those lorries, look –
the broken wagons lie.
A forge, for shoeing; mouldy tack,
hung on a sooty hook.

Dad said *I rode the horses home,
my legs stretched straight.* His walk
is stumbling, now. No child
could shift the great weights
on the ground. But see that tarry sack,
so leather-stiff – Grandpa heft a full one
on his back, and never flinched,
eyes rimmed black and fiery red,
his face a map of worry, lines
stained inky blue, like seams of coal.

For us, two weeks of wild delight,
nights sunk deep in feathers, three-a-bed.

Strange territory

A mile across fields to sea,
light years from where we lived before,
we lie in our granite redoubt,
and we look out.

A mist rolls in from the tangled moor,
wet-blankets the house. Beneath the mist,
the land writhes with life
like maggots on meat;
fox and shrew and feral cat.
Such a silent stalking and pouncing, such
a scuffling and scurrying, so much
blood and casual death.

Sun appears, mist clears.
A sudden buzzard, on a post.
His cold eye calculates as we flow
over soaking grass – then launches into
wind-washed air, seal into sea;
flip flop flaps away.

A thousand years ago,
that same round field; and women stood
as I stand now, searched the land for
strangers, lovers, food.
A standing stone points back.

When night comes,
roundly chewing in the round field,
a solitary stray beast's dark bulk
patiently waits for the farmer's call
back to the indifferent herd, the dirty stall.

Still it ain't over

We have taken the last card from the pack,
laid down the losing hand,
considered last month's stars
that failed to warn us of
the creek we now drift into.

And still it ain't over.

We are all through considering
the runes, the cast die, the way the sticks fall,
eating the crumbled cookies,
digesting the hat.
The cup has arrived at the lip.
The many slips and the hatched chicks
Have all been counted.   And still.

Nothing for it
but to uncross our fingers, ditch
the rabbit's foot, walk under ladders,
kick the black cat, send for the fat lady,
say boo to a goose.

Stepmother's tale

He was a banded offer:
want him, get her too.
She grizzled for her sainted mother.

Three's a crowd. God knows I tried.
He didn't want the bother.
I took a course in parenting.   She cried.

Drove me quite demented,
with her snow white, black and red.
I heard the rumours: *squatting in
a house with seven men*.
He blamed me, slept in the spare bed.

Even the mirror lied. The fairest. *She.*
You bet I wished her ill.
The rest you know about: the fatal fruit,
the glass box on the hill.

Stars

In the pinching-poor drabness of Britain at war
When life was on ration, and down at the school
Our teachers controlled us with rod and with rule –
They dangled a carrot: a little gold star.

Transported for ever, to heaven or hell
By those stars. Silver labelled us "good", "getting there",
With black for the feckless, who just didn't care –
And no star at all for the never-do-well.

We struggled for silver, we prayed for a gold,
While a quite different star, in the Ravensbruck night
Was falling, was dying, was fading from sight –
On a child's ragged sleeve, in the pitiless cold.

Singing in the harvest

Post-war poverty hung like a bad smell
on that hand-me-down home.
But even here, sometimes, we sang.

And what did we sing, by the
crazed stone sink, washing the dishes
and putting away? You'd think
our shiny council schools, all high ideals,
would teach the *lieder* – but we sang
a song more real to us, within our reach.

The jingles on the never-never box
told us of a brave new-minted world,
ours for the buying.
Is yours a Hovis home?
We thought so. Bought so.
Butter's best. Make mine a Mackeson
(and sod the rest).
We sang a hymn to plenty every night:
Omo adds bright bright brightness
– right? Wash your face in Lux – you'll be
fresh as the moment when the pod
goes pop –
hey, wait a minute, stop!
Never had it so good? Never had it at all,
but, shucks, we're trying. *Go Shell?*
Sure thing – but send a bloody car as well.

These work-songs for the poor
showed us what was waiting,
just beyond the door.
We want it! Give us more!

Presumed innocent

The apple was framed. Look, here in The Book:
it says *fruit* (non-specific), *the fruit of the tree.*
No mention of apple. Ask Adam, ask Eve.

Was any fruit, anywhere, ever more blameless?
Fat cheeks the colour of sweet summer grass,
tinged with an innocent blush, like a virgin,
round as a robin, as spotless as linen –
was *this* the temptation that started the rot?

And the things you can *do* with it!
Clean your sharp teeth with it, crunch it up, chew it,
drown it in toffee, or choke it with sugar;
bake it for hours in a puddle of butter –
bite the white flesh of it, suck out its heart.

But down in the garden, see, drowning in mist,
the cankerous tree, with the serpent entwined,
dying before you; and there on the ground,
storm ravaged, corrupted – the windfalls, fermenting,
tempting the wasp and the rootling swine.

Pre-nup

Don't ask:
what will I get when love is dead?

Ask instead, could you use his toothbrush?
Share his loo? Does he snore in bed?
Or fart, or scratch his head?
When you are safely wed, will he take
a drink, or four, or more? Will he be sick?
Knock you flat? Run to fat?

These are the devil's details. So
before you touch with the ten foot stick
or buy the poked pig, or endure
some leisurely repenting in
those ever-afters, ask

Does he wear his socks too long? In short
will he shirk the washing up? Live for sport?
Admit he's wrong?

Before you swap the rings, find out
if work is in his scheme of things.
Will he save, and share his pay, or
throw it all away, while you slave
till your dying day?

My friend, before the knot is tied
in the chain with the ball, discover –
Does your lover mean to mow the grass,
scratch his arse; will he wash his hands
before he handles you? Put the seat down
on the loo? Does foreplay turn him on?
Or is he in-out-off-sleep-gone?

Does he change his underclothes, or
pick his nose; or does he (frankly) smell?

Don't say – *oh what the hell!*
It's love, true love, and love's enough –
If push came to shove
could you use his toothbrush?

Well?

Nasty, British & Short

His tattoos swear he loves his mum,
his kids, his team, the wife:
the knuckles tell a very different tale.

In theory, you might admire
that squat Churchillian shape.
But this bloke lacks the way with words,
the cash, the posh, patrician pals.
His war is sport.

A grunt on legs, this Grant –
fat fingers jutting up (reversed).
The look that says *you want some, mate?*
The lack of hair, and grace.

Bulldog walks with Doberman,
bred for strife. One word out of place,
and he's upfront, and dishing out
the blood and sweat, the tears.

Feeling brave? Then face the lout
foursquare; say: *do your worst.*
On second thoughts,
best leg it. You can't win.
All wicked things that walk the earth
are in that face, that grin.

Virtual husband

When I wake, and when I lay me down
he's there, projected on
the pillow next to mine:
Beckham – or someone very like.

Skilled in the art of love, he waits
between my mind's clean sheets,
and sings the Song of Solomon.

His eyes are closed. My eyes are wide.
He is a thing of light, and lightly loves.
He kisses with the kisses of his mouth.

We feed on figs and wine.
Honey is under my tongue,
and look, his belly is a heap of wheat.
My beloved … O my beloved …

Here within this too real house
grouted, sanded, pointed, painted,
oiled and cleaned, drained, dusted,
scoured and greased
by someone else,
he waits.

My nose discovers spikenard and myrrh,
and cinnamon and cloves, and scent of musk.
He lies all night between my breasts
And feedeth among the lilies

Monkeys

The monkeys in the zoo
that's scarcely a zoo at all
– more a scattering of fields –
sit, hunched and bored
in the light rain.

In the landscape,
that's not really a landscape
– more a smattering of huts –
one big female grooms another,
while another picks at her.

Ropes add a jungle touch.
A single tree leans, lifeless.
They hang from it like fruit.
A listless infant dangles from
its mother's teat.

Do not approach the animals says that sign,
but nonetheless we do.
Do not feed the animals says this sign,
But still we stretch out hands weighed down
with inappropriate food –

until the big male stirs
and, as if in sleep,
moves purposefully towards us
over the dirty grass.

Landscape with ashes

Across a winter sea,
waves sluggish as oil,
slow and reluctant we come

to the island
yellow and black,
and the glistening beach.

The boat dumps its load
like litter, slinks away
from the desolate chill.

Day reduced to its essence.
Only this beach, this time
and a life in my hands.

I walk to the favoured spot
beyond the sands,
scatter him on the land.

Journey

Together we walked in the snow,
my beautiful girl and I.

Would you rather I kept these things secret?
she asked, as we set our feet
in the white snow, in the nothing but snow.
I said *Yes, yes, please spare me the facts* –

And we stopped beneath the magnolia, saw
the first of the blossoms, rusty with frost.
Looked back at our tracks behind us there,
criss-crossed, dark, in the white snow.

Interviewing Rose

They lead me to a room within a room
within a room. And there she is.

Tongue tied, I choke on words.
Relax, I tell myself, *she's only human.*
She takes my hand. I shake.
Turn on the tape. The tape. Tape.

The warder drops *Hello*, and slips the lock,
and sighs: she's heard this tale before.
I fall into these spaniel eyes.

Solid as suet, basin cropped,
she could be someone's mum. She is.
How? I want to ask, and *why?*
but I'm afraid. Incest, murder, torture, rape,
behind a very ordinary door.

Begin where you began, I say at last,
with childhood. Fat tears
score her cheeks. I scramble for
a tissue, cigarettes.
When I met Fred –
she's in control. Control. Control.
Choke. Gag. Tape. Lock. Start.
The tape records her cries.
So many dead.

In the Roman manner

Now we have heard the singular news,
let's plan it together,
like the good citizens we are.

Music, yes. Both are agreed on that.
A meal of – what? Something light and rare.
And wine, yes. We are agreed on that.

It will be winter, we will both be old.
A cold, bright day, in early afternoon.
We'll stroll into the garden, say hail
then farewell, to the dropping sun.
Afterwards we'll wander, arm in arm,
back to the warm room, and the music.

We place the letters by the jug
of winter roses. Spread the white cloth
on the floor, place pillows for each head.
We came, we saw –

This is the Roman, the best way to die.
Hand in hand, eyes dry,
we talk in a dead language.
Amat amas amo, te saluto – goodbye.

Ed, unvisited

Ed's unwelcome in the Trauma Ward.
We sick, we horizontal wounded women,
leave off glaring at each other, glare at him.

It's bad enough, we think, as one,
without some strange bloke, staring.
But Ed's not looking – floating just below the ceiling,
high on Class A drugs, and drifting.

Drink and drugs and drifting brought him here.
That, and the wrong woman. Three men warned him
Come back, and you're dead.
Moths, flames, who listens?

He wakes. *Scuse me, hen*, he begs,
his low Glaswegian croak a shadow on the wall.
The nurses tend him, warily.
Any chance of a drink?

Twenty three, he claims: not years, but broken bones.
His life is one long breakage.

Now we watch him yellowing. No visitors, just doctors,
and, at last, a policeman, come to call.

House clearance

Lot One:
child's cot (1950's), baby clothes (patched).
Tricycle, bicycle (puncture kit attached).

Lot Two:
miscellaneous vinyl, including Elvis (scratched).
Scooter helmet. Hockey stick. School books (boxed).

Lot Three:
hair curlers, hand mirrors, tarot cards (hexed).
Incomplete edition of Victorian novels (foxed).

Lot Four:
suitcase. Teach-yourself-a-Foreign-Language (text)
Postcards, rucksack, views of Bucharest.

Lot Five:
children's clothing, various, boys and girls (mixed).
Football strip, ballet outfit, jodhpurs (ripped).

Lot Six:
dinner service (hand thrown). Crystal glasses (chipped).
Collection of theatre programmes. Opera glasses
(cracked).

Lot Seven:
single bed. Dining chair. Photographs (distressed).
Tea-chest-full of paperbacks (poetry, obsessed).

Lot Eight:
Curtains

Has everybody gone?

His voice, thin as a silk scarf,
attempts to penetrate two doors.
Fails.

Tea would be nice.

A sour smell
announces his arrival
after the soft shoe shuffle
down the hall,
a journey long as Africa.

He'd be glad to talk
but no-one listens.
Stout girls in uniform
dump him in a chair
continue their rough chat
He never. He did. Men.

He gets his tea at last.
Weak stuff in a mug,
with the wrong kind of milk.

Hard living

Look at the girl, look at the mother –
don't stare.
The girl not yet fourteen, but big
and knowing, sly. The mum?
Finished, fat. Grey, greasy hair.

Down on the farm
that teeters on the edge
of cliffs and bankruptcy,
they live among a plague of cats,
a clutch of cock-eyed hens.
Grey curtains, never closed.
Sign in the yard, *eggs'n'spuds.*
No-one stops to buy.

The father? Watch him as he ploughs,
a distant smudge.
The sea's right there.
He'd throw a stone and hit it but
his eyes must trudge ungenerous land,
mind on his tea and his bed.

Nobody comes down the cow-splat lane.
Nobody goes. Nose out, keep out.
Strangers about.

Holding the line

They train a lifetime, for this.
You think it's easy, working up
such fury every morning, over tea?

Those spit and polished views they cling to –
love of Empire, anything Imperial:
ounces, pounds – in short,
the penny-pinching world
they once belonged to.

Angry old men muster in clumps
in pubs, in parks, faces red
as an old map. They bark their greetings,
wear their years like medals,
nurse old wounds, call out the daily roll:
Ted's gone, dropped in the night – poor soul.
They curse his luck, the times.

Each loss hardens resolve.
They are the righteous Few. *Buck up,*
they tell themselves, as they
stump, blinkered, through
this alien world, stone deaf
to every sound that does not suit,
fired by gin and brimstone.

Don't give an inch of ground!
Their last, sad victory. Don't give!
Not love, nor money, credit, time, an inch.

Freedom fox

Out in the meadow, white and winter-bare,
a far off farm-dog barks; the moon leaks light.
Stand very still, and see the sudden flare
of something thwart, untameable, this night.
He'll never be your friend, not he, nor mind
your human-tainted bait. Alert, in haste,
he crosses frost-encrusted earth, to find
some long-dead creature's corpse, more to his taste.

The fox is free! Like fire, see him run
the red and dangerous road. He heeds no laws.
Consumes whatever moves, braves trap and gun,
to shake the chicken world in bloody jaws.
You cannot lead him quietly to death,
like that poor tethered dog, man's so-called friend;
you'll have to hunt him down, to his last breath,
and watch, ashamed, as freedom meets its end.

Flotsam

The dirtiest beach in England
makes it hard to love dogs,
drinkers of Coke, scoffers of chips.

It's lunchtime, and the shabby winter sun
shambles across the sky. A wind from Siberia
seeks our bones. We hunch against it.

The shelter we cannot use
makes it hard to love lovers. See the walls,
full of sour slanders – who shagged, who sucks –
the wooden floor is awash with evidence.

On me like tar, sticky and persistent,
the melancholy of the out-of-season
hard-to-love town by the sea.

Fighting mad

In the shrunk heart, hurt –
energy rips across stretched eyes,
like lightning in the night.
The spark ignites – phht!
Spit sizzling on hot iron.
So fast the pressure mounts,
the mind's engine cracks –
flings nuts, bolts of words.
Everyone ducks for cover as
riotous blood breaks out,
thuds in the brain. Hands snap
into clubs, slap-bang-knock-clout,
punch to the floor, then
kick, kick, relief kicks in
as the strain drains out
through the booted foot the bunched fist
into the punch-bag flesh.
Feel how his shout, her scream, cool
his pounding blood, her blood a balm.

Then
 the slow walk back to calm.

Ending it

When a man stands on the edge of a cliff, looks down,
and sees on the shore below the anxious crowd,
and *jump, jump, jump* they holler, urgent and loud,
for the wind and the sea's clamour have carried away
the *don't don't don't* that should have been there; and say
he's the kind of man who always does what he's told –
then he'll spread his arms like wings, let go his hold,
and fly
        and for three long seconds he'll like it fine.

Do not waste time wondering how or where
or what path it was that led him, finally, here;
enough to know it was steep and stony and bare,
and the roar that he thought was the sea is now in his ears.
And anything's better than taking the dirt road back,
now that a light is dawning, out of the black.

Changing matter

One of those summer days when
heat shimmers over granite flags,
and babies, fractious as old men,
stiffen in your grasp,
leaking tears and worse.

One of those fried-egg-on-pavement days
when roads melt underfoot,
and butter turns in the dish.

On such a day as this
matter moves from
solid to liquid to smoke and air.

Old ladies choke and fall upon
slippery park benches,
loosening collars,
puffing cheeks.

Marriages bend and break
like iron in the forge,
and women lie on beds half-clothed,
praying for the relief of rain.

Calling for mother

Sophie sits in Belfast-bitter cold
in the outside lav, and listens to
the beast beyond. Bug-eyed,
she sees its breath smoke up
beneath the rotten door,
seeking her tender slippered feet,
which tremble there
above the concrete floor.

Her heart bangs drums
in her chest; her pinched face stares
at the rusty bolt that's all there is
between herself and death. She screams
Mum! Mum! Mum! Mum!
As loud as she can, *Mum! Mum!*

And it's black outside, and the wind rips,
threatening snow, and Sophie knows
a cobweb spreads above her head,
where a spider squats
big and black as a Bogside crow,
so she daren't stay, and she daren't go –

and she screams and screams
Mum! Mum! Mum! Mum!
at a far off woman, who will not come.

Bowerbird

He made a rainbow on the forest floor:
a flounce of flowers, coloured stones, small flags
of shining rag; paper, berries, foil –
with him in his outlandish finery,
dancing attention, drawing her in.

His song, translated, said: I've made
all this for you, my flighty dear;
a bower so beautiful
you'll never want to leave.
Come be my love, live with me here.

She stood bedazzled by the door,
this small grey bird, and as he danced,
allowed his twice-told tales to fill her ear.
She tried his nest for size, and was entranced.

He brought no more bright stones.
Instead he kept the world away. Be dutiful –
it's all for your own good, she heard him say.

When hours, days, weeks, had passed
and with them all her chicks, her hopes, his song –
she fluttered, shook him off, the way
a dog shakes water; caught the flare
of flowers in the sun. Was gone.

Birth battle

This is our war: the women's war.
Like old soldiers, outgunned
by nature, we birth survivors
slump in comforting groups,
relive each moment, tell of suffering borne,
how blood ran, flesh was torn.

How did we get into this?
As men get into war,
with dumb, unthinking confidence
till we learn sense, too late.

Oh, the slow coming to truth
through terror no drug could ease,
as we go over the top, no turning back
wave on wave, and us alone
in the hot shock of it. Through pain
beyond pain, singing our strange songs,
cursing our sex, his sex,
the sex that brought us here,
roaring *never again*!
we yell goodbye to youth.

After, injured inside, outside,
ripped, stitched, shorn;
we battle hardened troops, relieved
to be alive, limping homeward go.
Soldiers, mothers; we have crossed the line.
And though in time we will forget
(clinging to glory and the kids,
our trophies won) we're never again the same
as those, our lost, our former selves,
in that untested time.

All things being equal

I'm the last one you'd choose
to ease a lamb into life. But there it was:
me, the farmer, and the fat moon,
up and about on the farm.

It was on with my town shoes
and out in the night.
There, in the barn, the ewe made a noise
never heard from a sheep before;
enough to break a wolf's heart.

Crash course in the midwife's art.
I straddled the sheep's fat flanks,
gripped tight; stroked her camel's nose,
cried out *Push, push, good girl,*
breathe deep, one more for me!

We struggled and roared,
rumps in the air, shades of the two-backed beast.
Stiff legs poked through slime,
then out in a rush,
a blood streaked bag of meat.
We stared, shocked,
me and the ewe together.

Time
hung
suspended.

Then
Hallelujah!

Jerked to life,
shivered and mewed and rocked
on watery legs, scrambled and fell
and made it ...

The staggering ewe licked warmth
with her mothering tongue.
I stroked her broad, hard back,
bleated *Good girl! Well done*!

St Michael's Mount

How like a breast, jutting from the sea,
garlanded with weed, exposed
by teasing waves. Amazonian, you might say

in its singularity. Over the cobbles at low tide
figures cross as if walking on water,
drawn to the breast, as a child

seeks softness. Because it is so like a breast,
one breast, disturbing in its femininity,
defying the natural order of things,

generations have scored it with tracks –
graffiti on the image of a nude;
confused our sense of it with tales

of giant's hearts, cocked it with cannons,
hallowed it with monks, ordered it with lords,
and named it after a man.

Stuttering through Sparkbrook

On the Number Four, I peer through grime
at supermarket saris, flaring under
artificial light. Bird-of-paradise blue,
shocking pink.

In Curry Heaven, plastic chairs
wait for better times, posters offer haj.
Next door's internet cafe
(Sheikhspeare Global), offers access
to Bengal, Somalia, Kandahar, Kashmir.
On the seat in front, an Irishman
Mournefully sings of mountains,
curses no one, everyone.
A six-foot Rasta stoops, admonishes.
Hey maan, too early for that.

Anonymous in black, I shed the bus,
beetle home, head down.
Neighbours strain charity-shop tweeds
over salwar-shamiz, against
the biting Brummie wind.

Back down the road in Solihull
A woman walks her Pekingese.

Incident at Birmingham New Street

She waits for the Glasgow train,
winding its way to the West Country.
As she waits, she talks to her child
in a voice you could cut with a skian dhu.
Pure Scots. *See yer grandpa soon, eh?*
Her sari – pure Punjab. The train arrives.

Her bearded, turbaned father
lowers himself with care, as if from a mule.
She runs along the platform
straight to his arms. Her mother, tearful
in tartan, a chorus of daughters and aunts,
cascade from the train. They crowd round,
press tenners in the child's hand. In the air,
endearments in Punjabi swarm like bees.

A whistle blows.
Everyone screams but the child,
who quietly considers the cash.
The father gives commands,
and the family trail him onto the train
in a skirl of silk, off to a wedding in Plymouth.

All but the girl, and her son.
She's a Brummie, now, and she stays here.
Her heart is as full as a haggis.
Her pain as sharp as a thistle.
I'm sae hamesick fer Scotlan',
she whispers to the indifferent boy,
prising the cash from his fist, in return for a sweet.

Beating the Bounds

Down here, they Beat the Bounds.
On each Ascension Day, they congregate,
walk the parish edge,
and Beat the Bounds.

I'm curious. *We like to keep the old ways up,*
says one. *Why don't you come along
and watch?*

I do, and stand there fidgeting
among the incomers, the trippers
and indifferent passers-by,
while furious blood-red farmers
stamp about, beating the earth
with willow sticks,
marking the boundary of their
long lost territory, their long lost land.

Fishy town

Here lives a man who slithers back and forth
between two wives, one up the lane,
one down. They meet sometimes,
these hooked and gutted fishwives,
bubbling oaths, as Bible Christians
once faced out the Primitives.

Butcher, baker, chippie, fish-shop, bank
and fourteen heaving pubs, sustain
a vinegary town, where men,
fresh down from Defra, sometimes find
themselves and all their quotas
toppled headlong in the quay.
They don't do romance here.
Broken bottles, shells, a woman's lacy pants,
reef the gutters, an all-week memory
of hell-up Saturday night. Secrets salt the air.

Hands boiled red as lobsters
make a fist, give the fishy finger;
eyes like slate, or fathoms-deep and dark,
watch and wait. And then the sudden strike:
it's payback-time, among the weeds.

Up lanes, shoals of children flash across
the cobblestones, gape at strangers, disappear
as one, into their tiny rocky homes.
A man's voice fills the stair: *not stinkin fish again!*
I told you, woman, no more stinkin fish!

41 uses for a dead church

Arts centre, luxury flats, theatre, house,
drop-in centre, furniture warehouse, supermarket, pub,
women's refuge, asylum centre. Somewhere to
graffiti on. Laundromat, sanctuary, tourist centre, mosque,
concert hall, rehearsal room, shooting gallery, crèche.
Bat sanctuary, war memorial. Pigeon roost. Loo.
Somewhere nice and private to make love.

Target practice, rehearsal room, video rental, store.
Backdrop for videos and horror movies, squat.
Source of antiques. Subject of a history project (dull).
Non-denominational, politically correct, faith lodge (full).
Spiritual centre. Mission centre. Senior Citizens' Club.
Gymnasium. Doss-house, tax loss, joke.
Somewhere dry to shelter from the rain.

The naked poetry reading

The ladies of the
Penzance Poetry Appreciation Society
claiming inspiration from Byron and Burns
decided to expose themselves
for the benefit of
the Distressed Poets' Benevolent Fund.

Breasts and buttocks shapely as a sonnet
rude as a limerick
round as a rondeau,
natural as Wordsworth
and as free as verse
were noticeably absent from the scene.
Instead, a McGonagall of misshapen flesh
was exposed to the pitiless scrutiny of critics.

They did the reading twice.
The first time to the usual audience
of thirteen women and a dog.
The second (word got round)
to a packed theatre in Truro.

Learned gentlemen from Oxbridge
asked the question: *Why?*

It is a poet's duty to expose the truth,
declaimed the chair, naked as a newborn,
sans even glasses, trailing clouds of glory.

The seven ages of words

After Mama, Dad, first namings –
Dog and Doll and Me Me Me

comes who? and why? and what?
and where? and then

I *want*, you *give* me (infinite)
from years six to ten.

Next, puberty, a time of
Screamers! Forward slashes/Dashes –
every word in **bold** and **CAPS** –
which mercifully fades
and in its place,

the pale, poetic silences of love,
the sudden lexicon of words
they know, you don't.

Their world talks now,
through faint, and far off
voices on the phone, concealing
everything except their irritation,

until they find you,
sideways in the chair, with
someone spooning words
out of your mouth.
Sadly, they call your name.
Mama. Your turn for
baby language, now.

Alphabet man

On those nights when
my head is bursting blood,
I take myself to open spaces,
feel the air, breathe free.

Amazed, how many
run the midnight roads,
skipping in the lights of crawling cars.
Who cares for them? I do.
I take good care of them.

Sometimes I catch one
on the swings, alone.
Push us mister, give us a push
they shout. I know their games.
Soon they're tracing out
the dark of my tattoos, each one
a letter in its own red heart.

Do I have to spell it out?
I bring them presents, comics, fun,
remember all their names.
They read me. Love me.
Trust me, every one.

Canute

Marooned, we cling
to rocks, consider tides and times,
the drowning sun.

Last week our tree fell down.
This week they forecast floods,
and we fill sandbags on
the clamant beach.

Life is elemental, and it suits
our new philosophy. Up country,
leaders change or try to change
by force or by consent.
Tyrants crouch in holes,
politicians boss the waves about.

Wouldn't it be great if we
could just turn back the clocks? He says.
His eyes lament my face,
I read between his lines.

Days slide.
The sun bobs up again, the clock goes round.
The tide comes in, goes out,
without our help,
without our by-your-leave.

The yoga positions of unrequited love.

The meercat
Eight, he said. Outside the station.
Don't be late. Or was it nine?
The other gate? You peer. You wait.
No, honestly, I'm fine.

Springs eternal
Sit astride the bleak world blind,
your lyre in hand.
Say while there's life there's –
Tell yourself he'll leave his wife.
She'll understand.

The props (basic)
Fags, booze, pills of various kinds.
Long-suffering family, friends.
One night stands. Lost weekends.

The crushed soul
Recite this mantra –
wished, washed up, squashed, dashed
Mope and moan, until dementia.

The cocked ear
On permanent alert for
the stubbornly silent phone.
Against all sound advice,
call him. Twice. He's clearly not alone.

When all's said, retire to bed.
Pull the blankets over your head.
Play dead.

Listing

Because I have acquired the rarity value
that comes with a long history;
because I am corrugated,
with a fine grey patina –

the Society for the Conservation
Of Rundown English Women (SCREW)
is attempting to have me listed.

They consider my mossy overhang,
my bulging sides,
to be ripe for preservation.
They admire the sturdy way
I have endured so many storms.

They fear that someone else
with doubtful taste
will turn up, take me over,
insist on radical dentistry,
Brazilian waxing, nip and tuck.
Atkins.   Botox.   Even a boob job.
And all the charm of a certain antique style
of woman would be lost.

Now I have been offered
to the National Trust.
Sightseers crowd my door,
curious to see what happens when
a woman simply grows old.

Crash

Black Monday, Terrible Tuesday,
and now Effin Awful Friday.

Like a bear and a bull we watch our stock
plummet, soar, plummet.

Bonds break under the strain.
Gilts tarnish. Gelt vanishes.

Long-dates shorten, Shorts bust,
spreads close. Blue chips are down.

We are burned out, dumped,
hammered (but not screwed).

A pair of suckers, mullets, lilies;
trading insults, crunching numbers.

Lulled, gulled, taken to the cleaners,
put through the wringer,

Crashed out, cashed in, crushed and coshed,
wiped out, cleaned out, hung out to dry.

Boots

Eight hundred pairs of boots
stand easy on the White House lawn.

A Quaker protest, this,
in line with a belief in quiet, peace.
You'll find no oil, no blood, no sand
on these black boots.

Innocent working boots.
Put them on the right feet
and they'll walk a war,
kick a man to shape. Those laces
make a fine garrotte.
Nobody dances in boots like these.

You might decide they brought it
on themselves, those men
who ambled to the wrong
recruiting office, on the wrong
spring day, marched out
to their quietus.

A cold café, the three of us,

and the waiter asking *Are you the meat?*

No, I say. I am the plain vegetarian quiche,
bitter green salad with herbs, no dressing.
She is the Chateaubriand, *avec truffes.*
He is the well-hung game, marinaded in stout,
side order of chips.

      Who's for pudding? He asks.
No pudding for me, but she will have
Death by Chocolate, sprinkled with
hundreds and thousands.
He will have upside down pudding,
topped with full dairy cream.

      And to follow?
I will have coffee, strong, black, no sugar.
She will have latte, sponge fingers.
He will have Irish coffee,
brandy to follow.

They will be leaving early.
I will be picking up the bill.

Today we have breaking of hearts

The man devours the words,
buckles and slumps. Howls
in the space her clothes have
left behind. Pesters her friends.
Feels her slip away with the day,
somehow already lost. She, lost,
scours the strange town,
counts her change,
considers takeaway. Buys wine.

The man rattles around
the big house, cleans and closes
rooms. Drains wine. She shakes off
the rented room, moves on.
Makes ends, counts costs. He thinks
of endings. She considers meetings,
thinks again. Remembers acts
of kindness. Counts her friends.

The shrunk man spoons cold soup.
Lives small. She aches to the bone.
Neither can remember why,
or how, it ended, or began,
or if at all.

Beware of the dog

In the Chumchomping, leghumping,
blindleading, arselicking, shepherding,
heelwalking, lift-up-your-paw
and-shake-hands drooling heart
of a slavering slave of a dog –

curls what's left of the gene
of the Little Red
can'tseethewoodforthe

Wolf.   And it wants letting out.

Desire

Oh, my once love,
If we were to meet now, even as we are now,
in our sere, white, cautious middle age,
I swear in a moment we'd lie down together,
tenderly peel the years from one another,

and I would lead you back
through the memory of skin,

and we would become all skin.
And though we might not ask, for trembling
what we so often asked before –
which way now, which way?
at length our tongues and fingers would unearth
the old path back.

And I would moan, not as I moan now,
about the wind and weather,
but naked, shuddering, over and over –

and you would shout, and fall upon me,
not as the years fall on me now,
but as water falls, in a land without rain.